THE BREAKING
OF MYSELF

THE BREAKING
OF MYSELF

Carissa Rees

POETRY CHAPEL
PRESS

Copyright © Carissa Rees 2025.

All rights reserved. No part of this publication may be reproduced, distributed, or transmitted in any form or by any means, without prior written permission of the respective author.

Poetry Chapel Press
Brisbane, QLD, Australia
Cover Illustration: Copyright © 2025 Carissa Rees

The Breaking of Myself / Carissa Rees. -- 1st ed
ISBN 978-1-7642168-0-7

For those who find comfort in my words

*Brokenness is not the absence of love
but permission to be loved even more*

Contents

Discovery	1
Peculiar nothingness	2
End of autumn	4
The things I keep hidden	6
Realisation	7
Takes me back home	8
When you read my words	11
Healing process	13
March	14
Slow mornings	17
Blue/blew	19
Fingernails	20
Instead of running	22
Sacred spaces	24
To know me	25
Longing to leave	27
Collecting moments	28

Little perfects	30
Any less true	31
A picture book summer	32
Movement	34
My toes are dancing	37
Anger	39
Somewhat held together	41
When deciding	42
I've been the peacekeeper	45
My own demise	46
Once again	48
When I wake	51
Cartwheels	53
Ducks	54
Grass	56
The girl who glowed	57
Both can exist	59
Will it ever go away?	60

Spilling	61
Still hurting	62
Bolted shut	64
Continual saving	66
I do not need to worry	69
Haunted from hiding	71
Bottom line	73
A place for everything	74
The vase is bleeding	77
Prove me wrong	78
Until it sinks in	79
Self-deprivation	80
Yes	82
This too shall pass	84
Creating	87
I'm in a state of being	88
Sunken deep	89
My mind is a house	90

Progress	91
Letting tears learn	93
Sometimes it takes another	95
The art of notekeeping	96
Conversation with a friend	99
The depths in you	101
Closing the door	102
Being known	104
Pick me up	107
The Breaking of Myself	108
Unravelled	110
Balance along beams	112
There are no answers	113
Taking up space	114
My fear doesn't yield power	117
Immersed in sunlight	119
Raindrops	120
Underlying sadness	122

Discovery

At the beginning of the year
I vowed that I would take risks
and when I am doubting
I remind myself of this

that I would put myself in the unknown
experience the unexpected
learn what ignites my passion
what fuels my soul

and in the act of all this
will there still be a longing?
or will I have even more to long for?

Peculiar nothingness

With no agenda

    only d a n c i n g
    and s m i l i n g

at the peculiar

    n o t h i n g n e s s

that life brings

    when
        we let it

The Breaking of Myself

End of autumn

My colour leaves
as I collapse
like a leaf after fall
I can't get up

It's the end of autumn
and leaves let exhaustion
tell them
to 'rest'

the same way I listen to nature
I can listen to myself
and learn to lay down when my body aches
learn to listen

before   the   break

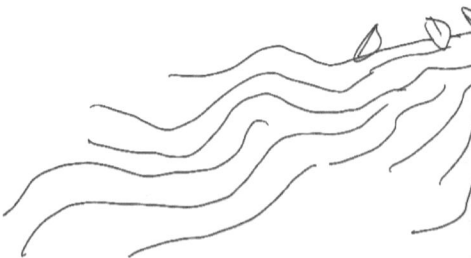

The Breaking of Myself

The things I keep hidden

I practice the words over and over
tomorrow comes
and we speak of anything but this

and I'm afraid
that I'm not real
and never have been

I can't confide
can't think of a time
in where I haven't told this lie

and going forward–how can I?
when you have only ever known
my disguise

Realisation

The things I want the most
are the things I fear the most
–being known

Takes me back home

These feelings i'll remember
for these places
takes me back home

to the first time you took my sorrow
and showed me
that *you* exist

and here
I am the tree planted by the waters
and you are the mountainside

the more I stay here
the more my branches grow
the more I stay here

the more *you* are my home

The Breaking of Myself

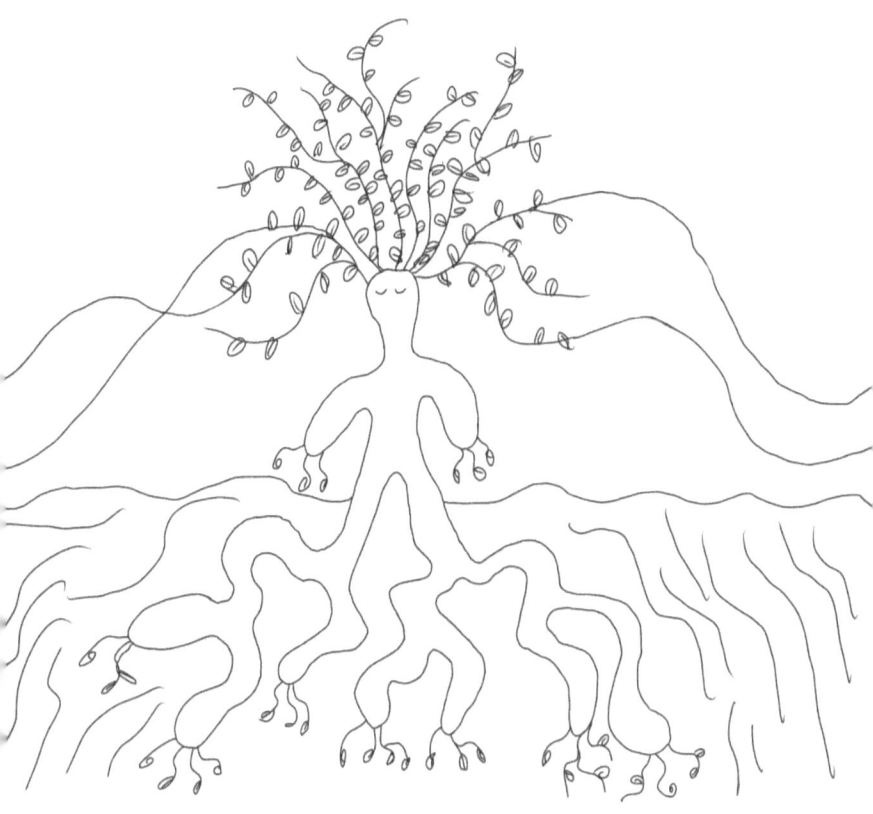

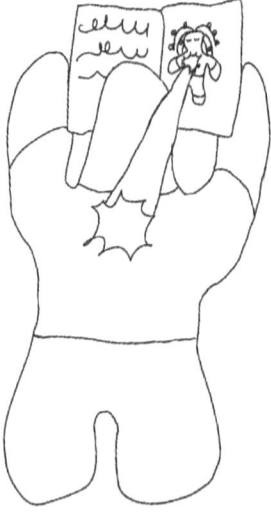

When you read my words

When you read my words
for the first time
remember how it was
when you knew me
when our souls spoke
at the same time
and it was like
nothing else was needed
but each other

Healing process

Paper is a place for wounds to bleed
for imprints of words never said aloud

Permission to seep deep into pages
a place where wounds turn into scars

The difference being:
the wound is the damage that's been done
-slow to heal

The scar is the story behind the wound
-a reminder of the healing

March

The month of March
was the month of misery
the month of unsustainability

my mentality
was not at its finest
and I was not at my nicest

if I could spend a million dimes
to not feel this way any longer
I would

for I withhold the truth
disguise it
so you won't recognise it

although, I want you to know

but I have hidden
too many
times

it is now a habit
I cannot
break

The Breaking of Myself

transparency
honesty
I need to try those things

allow myself
to speak
of what I deem
unspeakable

allow you to lean
into all i've kept
unseeable

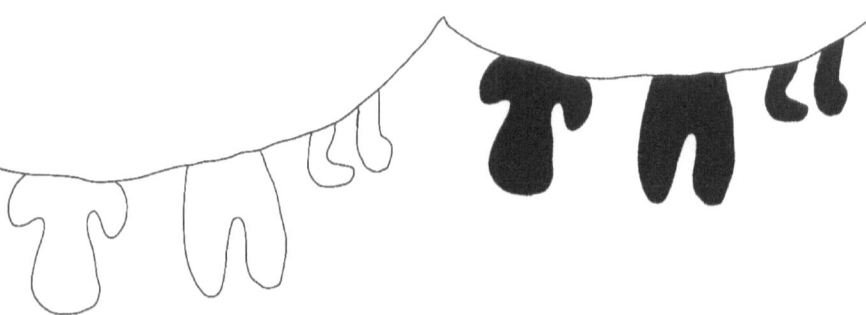

Slow mornings

I look forward to doing nothing
but clothing myself in the warmth of the sun
and seeing the movement
of shadows on
things nearby

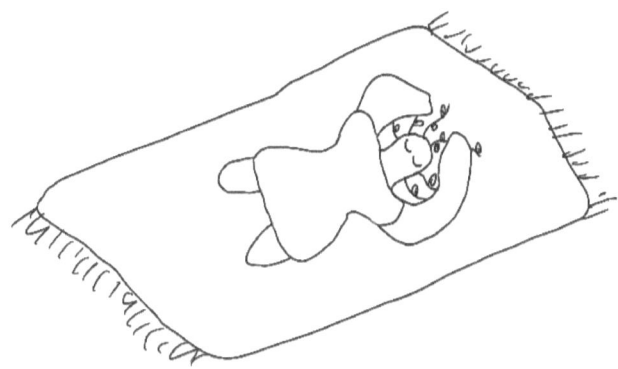

Blue/blew

I don't know if I like it here
like I thought I would

This *blue* I've been wearing
never seems to leave
unlike everything else

'Take me to the port'
I tell the driver
as my uncertainties *blew* over once more

I'll sail across the seas
and let the wind decide my fate
I don't want to be the decider
I don't want to be in this state

Fingernails

I love being slow
I let my nails grow
and in this time of being alone
I let my thoughts roam

I love it here,
with myself
and I am learning more and more
contemplating at the lake

what shall I do?
what shall I be?
nothing other than what I have been
with the possibility of even more

and now my fingernails at full length
have begun
to break

and so the process starts again
even though, I have learnt
I am never truly at the end

grow
break
repeat

the cycle is never complete

Fingernails

I love being slow
I let my nails grow
and in this time of being alone
I let my thoughts roam

I love it here,
with myself
and I am learning more and more
contemplating at the lake

what shall I do?
what shall I be?
nothing other than what I have been
with the possibility of even more

and now my fingernails at full length
have begun
to break

and so the process starts again
even though, I have learnt
I am never truly at the end

grow
break
repeat

the cycle is never complete

Instead of running

If only the kite would pick me up
so we can soar through the skies
despite the wind that blows against us

The Breaking of Myself

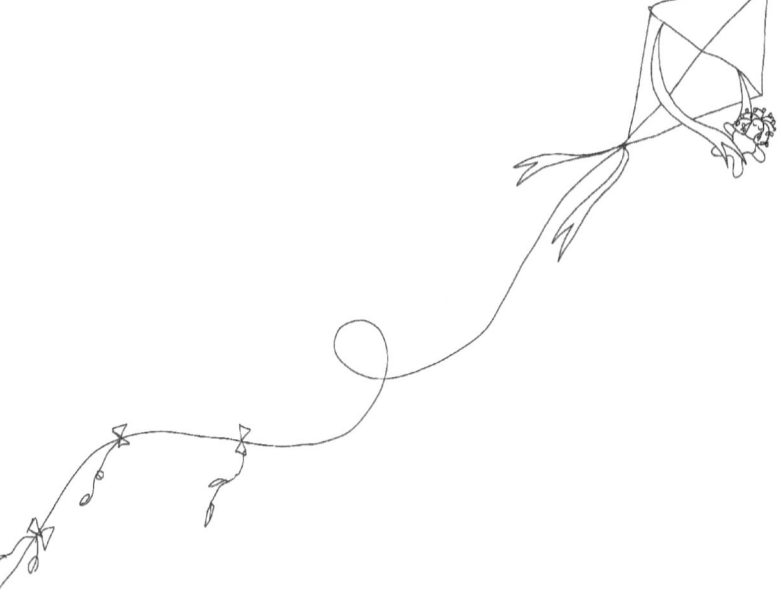

Sacred spaces

I wake to write
I sleep to dream
both of these so sacred
for in these spaces
-I grow

and in growing
I am able to be awake
I am able to dream dreams

To know me

Things I exist in:
the pillow
the glass of water
the book on the bedside
the breeze on a summers eve
Things that bring a sense of comfort.
That is what it is like to know me.

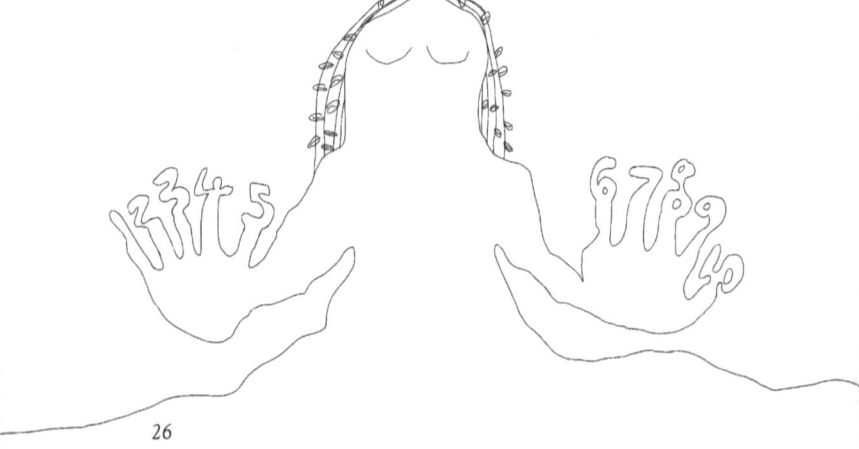

Longing to leave

This perfect place I live in
is still
not enough

Existing is effort
when I don't know what I'm existing for
I am only what I know
which is what I'm still trying to figure out

I count the days until I leave
I rewrite what I've already written
while I wait for my life to start
at this new place

But what if...
it has already
and I'm too lost
to even notice it

Collecting moments

I stop participating
and start observing
the world is slow
as if to let me notice
what would otherwise pass me by

I draw what I see
commemorate moments
as they should be
I use my gifts
to *honour*
who gave them to me

I fill these pages
with words
that express how my heart feels

I draw to remind myself
I am really here
I am really living

The Breaking of Myself

Little perfects

It all happens
In a single instance.

The fall

    of a

        gumnut,

the splash

    of a

        puddle.

I call these
little perfects.

Moments that seem so small
yet deviate my attention
to something bigger.

Any less true

The good things in my life
don't make my struggles any less true

A picture book summer

A picture book summer
consists of prancing through the streets
and stopping
to draw
every moment that I
admire

It's music that fits the moment
it's smiling while lying on the grass
and thinking how cute humans can be

It's observing
it's note taking
the colours that I see

It's allowing the world around me
to be noticed
to be the feature of my canvas

The Breaking of Myself

Movement

if we have these bodies

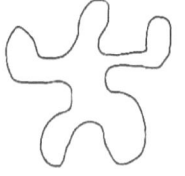

The Breaking of Myself

why aren't we *dancing?*

My toes are dancing

My toes are dancing
I am levitating
up
into the sky

That's no metaphor
I really am
flying

and if you don't believe me
you'll see me
out your window

I am beaming
I think I am now
part of the universe
in some way

I am the sunlight streaming
though the branches off trees
that make people
stop and stare

and wonder
about the beauty
that life can be

Anger

I must feel it completely
for if I don't
it only lingers

so I take my time
sit with it
say the thoughts I'd normally push away

I hate the process
how it feels I'm not making progress

but at least I am acknowledging
everything that's in me

for if I don't
I'm not deceiving anyone
but myself

Carissa Rees

The Breaking of Myself

Somewhat held together

reliant on my unreliability
adapted to my deficiency
at least my eyes don't bleed
like they used to
not because I got better
but because I got used to it

When deciding

Bound by circumstances
beyond my change

My heart wants one thing
my health another

Is the question:
Is it attainable?
or is my heart able?

The Breaking of Myself

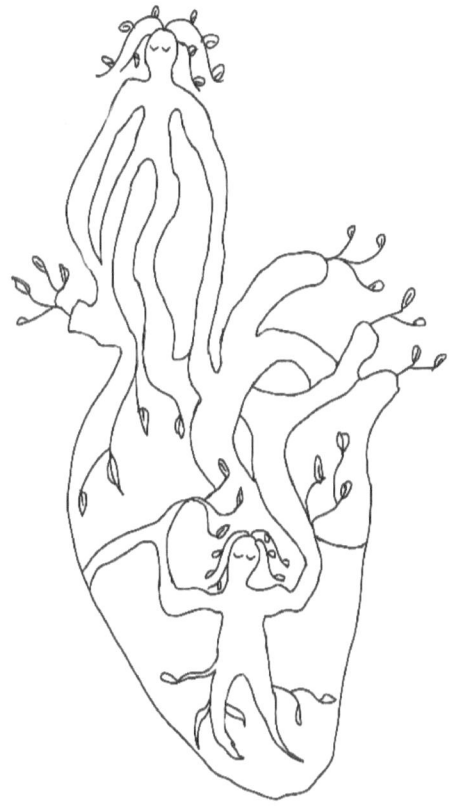

I've been the peacekeeper

I've been the picture
painting a thousand words
without saying anything

for with words I lose
lose who I am to you

and my act of leaving it all unsaid
has been the worst act of all
leaving me so insecure
that you don't even know me

like you did before

my silence no longer gives space for speech
my avoidance now confused with peace

so I write the words I am wanting to say
but of course they stay
on my silly little page

because silence offers me something
words can't
the protection that I will need
when you decide to leave

My own demise

These words
curated over the years
no longer carry meaning

these journals
hand crafted
were made to be burned

I too
just like my words
am ripped apart

for I am the paper
torn into pieces
before it's thrown into fire

and turned into ash

The Breaking of Myself

Once again

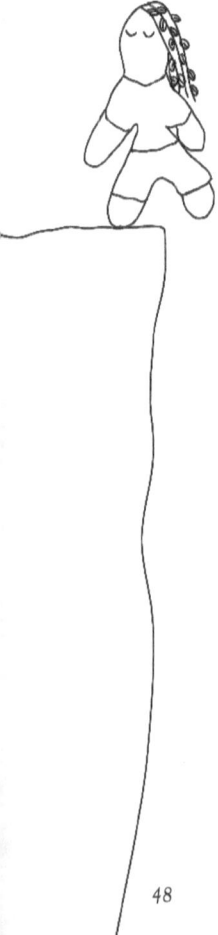

I had permission to be heard
           and turned it down
                      because I was
                              afraid

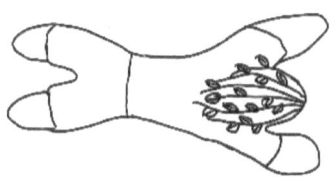

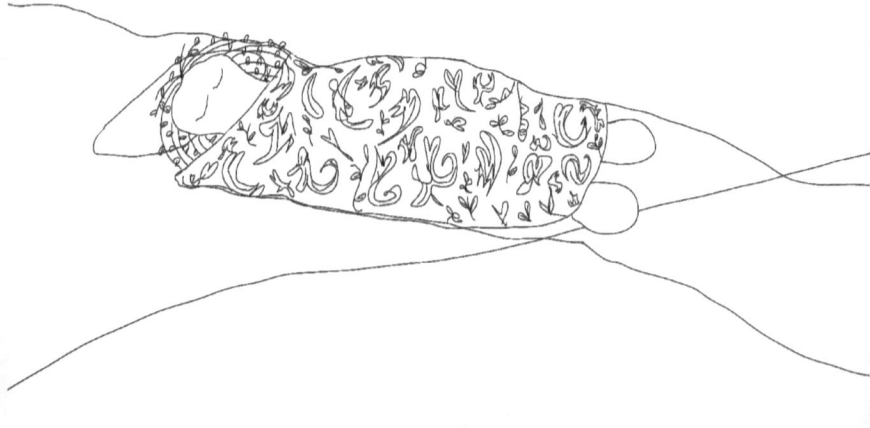

When I wake

I want to wake up and be excited to be alive
I want to wake up and feel healthy in my body
I want to wake up and be able to walk again
I want to wake up and feel happy

Cartwheels

My hands hit the sands
I fall
as laughter leaves my lips
in this failure to land

worries ease
as if to tell me
that this laughter is allowed
in my falling

and in this process
of not always
landing it

Cartwheels

My hands hit the sands
I fall
as laughter leaves my lips
in this failure to land

worries ease
as if to tell me
that this laughter is
allowed
in my falling

and in this process
of not always
landing it

Ducks

The ducks are sleeping

        beaks burrowed, under the sun

                i'll curl up as well

The Breaking of Myself

Grass

I listen to grass
as they whisper together
'growth takes time'–they say

The girl who glowed

She reached out to the sun
who filled her with awe and wonder
and as she began to dance
the feeling inside of her started to grow

and so did the flowers

Both can exist

My joy doesn't take away from my sorrow
my sorrow doesn't take away from my joy

Will it ever go away?

I don't know if it will ever go away
but I wonder
would I still think this deeply about it all
if it weren't for this pain?

Spilling

If I am not aware

emotions take the lead

    and I am

        spill
            ing

at the start of our speak

Still hurting

It's hard to look after myself
when I am the one who is hurting

The Breaking of Myself

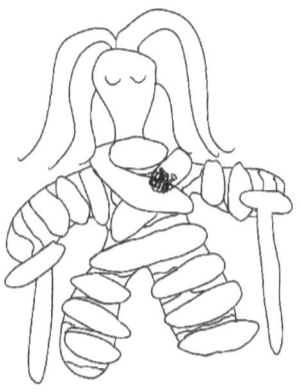

Bolted shut

I bolted my windows shut
so no air could get in
thought if I suffocated
it might enlighten me
that a near death experience
would cause an epiphany
and when I take that next
realised   breath
I would know what to do

The Breaking of Myself

Continual saving

I need you
I need saving
I need your promise
tell me what you want to tell me

. . . and I will listen

I do not need to worry

Right now
this feels eternal
but it won't be

I have fears
of what could occur
because of my past

but I won't let
what has happened
shape what will

for nothing is worse
than proclaiming a possible truth
over something

that has not happened yet

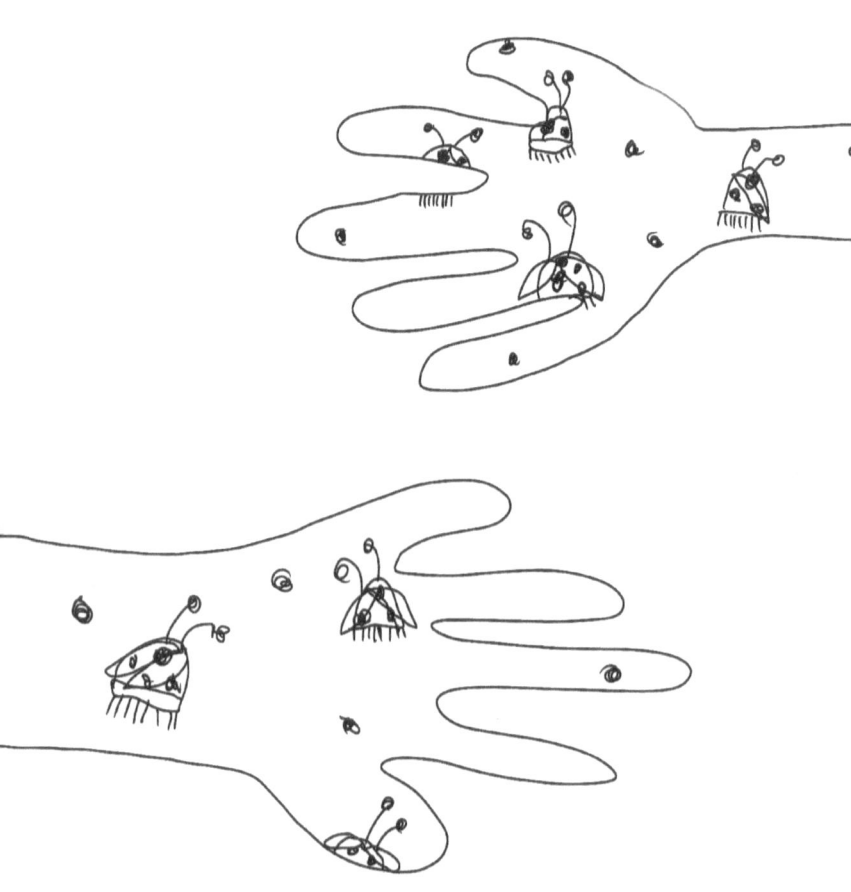

Haunted from hiding

Haunted from hiding
I feel like a lie
I'm unraw
the opposite of my writing
a fraud
and on the inside
there's a beetle
eating its way out
tears sting my eyes
I feel every bite

as usual, I say nothing

my silence is my suffering

Bottom line

I'm ill from my unendings
and there's nothing to be done
my body is decaying
as destruction comes undone

The bottom line is:
I am living in a battle that cannot be won

A place for everything

I fall into the fields
for this is my place
where I can be rested

and lately rage is the only thing that stops me
from being here
and it knows none else
but fear of being felt

so I extend the space

let my downfall take the place
inviting what I think I won't like
while I try not to run away

for emotions need to know
that they are safe
so that pain too can learn
it's allowed to be felt

for it's only when I am present
to what's within me
that I am present
to what's around me

and if anything
I have learnt
that everything
that feels limiting

just hasn't found it's place

The vase is bleeding

how can I heal
when my wounds have wounds
when water poured into the vase
bleeds through the cracks
when its my tears
that need holding
only they are falling
my weakness now ignoring

that it's *me*

the one who needs restoring

Prove me wrong

I fear I won't be loved
because of the parts I hate about myself
-prove me wrong

Until it sinks in

my pain does not define me. my pain does not define me.
my pain does not define me. my pain does not define me.
my pain does not define me. my pain does not define me.
my pain does not define me. my pain does not define me.
my pain does not define me.my pain does not define me.
my pain does not define me. my pain does not define me.
my pain does not define me. my pain does not define me.
my pain does not define me. my pain does not define me.
my pain does not define me. my pain does not define me.
my pain does not define me. my pain does not define me.
my pain does not define me. my pain does not define me.
my pain does not define me.my pain does not define me.
my pain does not define me. my pain does not define me.
my pain does not define me. my pain does not define me.
my pain does not define me. my pain does not define me.
my pain does not define me. my pain does not define me.
my pain does not define me. my pain does not define me.
my pain does not define me. my pain does not define me.

Self-deprivation

This well reserved demeanour
the side of me
that's now to you, so familiar
is not who I am

for I had youthfulness
a grin
more to me beneath
my skin

but it got up and left
the same day
my hopefulness drained away

and with it took the part of me
that I had learned to love

that took years of tending to
mentally mending over
the self-hatred
the pity

The Breaking of Myself

now only self-deprivation fills this void
that my self care is too small
to fill

for I am only
a corpse
of what once was

breathing without lungs
speaking without tongue

Yes

'Do you feel sick of it?'
'Are you tired?'
'Is it frustrating?'
'Are you on the outskirts?'
'Do you feel hidden?'
'Are you someone who hides?'
'Do you feel like a burden?'

I don't know if I feel outed or seen.

The Breaking of Myself

This too shall pass

help me to know, this too shall pass

pain [.?!!]

small compared to what is coming

The Breaking of Myself

―――――――――――――――――――   eternity

Creating

I create so I can feel, I feel so I can create

I'm in a
state of being

what if I removed the lens
of how I view my emotions
and just accept that

I am feeling

Sunken deep

like a weight
I have sunken deep
I just don't understand?
but if that's where I am
that's where you'll find me

how deep will you go
to save me?

My mind is a house

my
mind
is a house
that hasn't been
tended to. it's my only
companion and it has been
unwell, so I enter the rooms in my
head. the ones with curtains closed
which need the light on again, but hitting
the switch doesn't work when the room
doesn't know who she is without darkness and
bringing light is not so easy
when I'm full of insecurity
but my uncomfortability is
what needs attention. to face
what I hate. by taking time
to mend over all the things
that have only ever known
pretend. for it's in the mending
of this home that self-hate
turns itself into grace.

Progress

Things I am proud of:
- allowing myself to rest
- communicating my needs
- being honest

These are big things for me.

Letting tears learn

Sorrow has changed me
in a way nothing else
ever could

I used to avoid sadness
but feeling the blues
makes my understandings new

and I am burrowed
in deep with my emotions
the more I get to know them
the more I make sense

by giving what's inside me a name
and letting tears learn
that being seen
doesn't mean

shame

Sometimes it takes another

I am proud of her
her strength
how she stands with pain

I am proud of me
the perseverance in her
so I see it
in me

The art of note keeping

I reread the words
that were once my lifeline
the letter I wrote
for safekeeping

a reminder-of how far I've come
a reminder-to let go in the moment
it doesn't matter
in the long run

The Breaking of Myself

Conversation with a friend

'you don't need to worry about me'

                                                'I worry because I care'

Carissa Rees

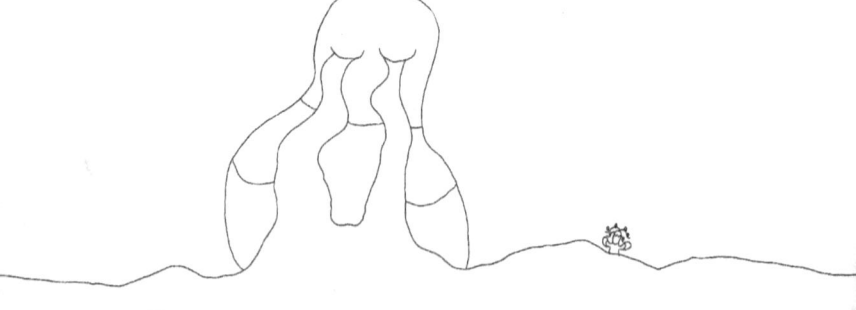

The depths in you

My sorrow is full
to the brim
that rivers
fall down my chin

this pain in me
I see in you
rivers down deep
flowing past your cheek

empathy forms in my pit
the place in me I thought
could not be reached

but by your tears I am taken here
for the depths in you
are seen in the depths in me

and this pain that lives
in the crevice of my soul
is now no longer alone

for compassion has found it
and calls it home

Closing the door

Shame lets himself in
but I get to tell him to leave

The Breaking of Myself

Being known

I choose
to let my care
be uncovered

fight the urge
to find my cave
and stay there

I want to be known
for my good
as well as my bad

to take off the layers
that i've tried so hard
to conceal

and let you hold
a piece
let you hold me

D e c o n s t r u c t e d

sharp at the edge
jarring at times

I *choose* to let you hold me

The Breaking of Myself

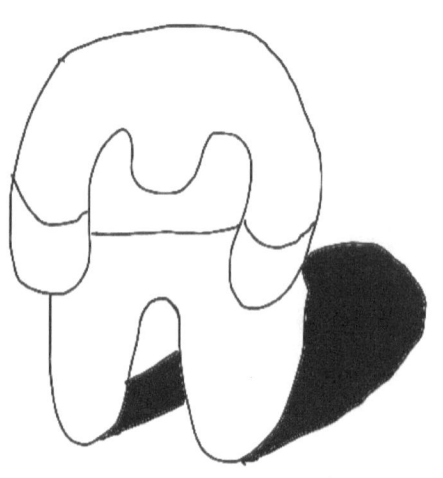

Pick me up

Pick me up
I've tried to be strong
and I am tired
I can only hold myself
like this
for so long

and that's okay,

because aren't we all
meant to be held
by another?

The Breaking of Myself

Finally I feel understood
I feel known
the darkest parts of me
are seen
and strangely I don't feel
ashamed
like I have been

I don't have to hide anymore
and this agony that is all consuming
does not define who I am

For it's in the breaking of myself
that I know
I am still loved

The Breaking of Myself

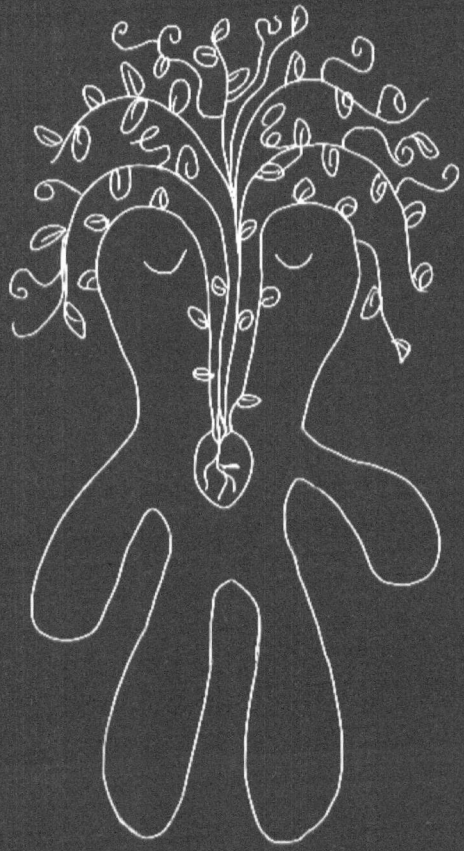

Unravelled

Once I am unravelled
I cannot stop
because it doesn't control me anymore
and I delight
in being

                    let

                                    loose

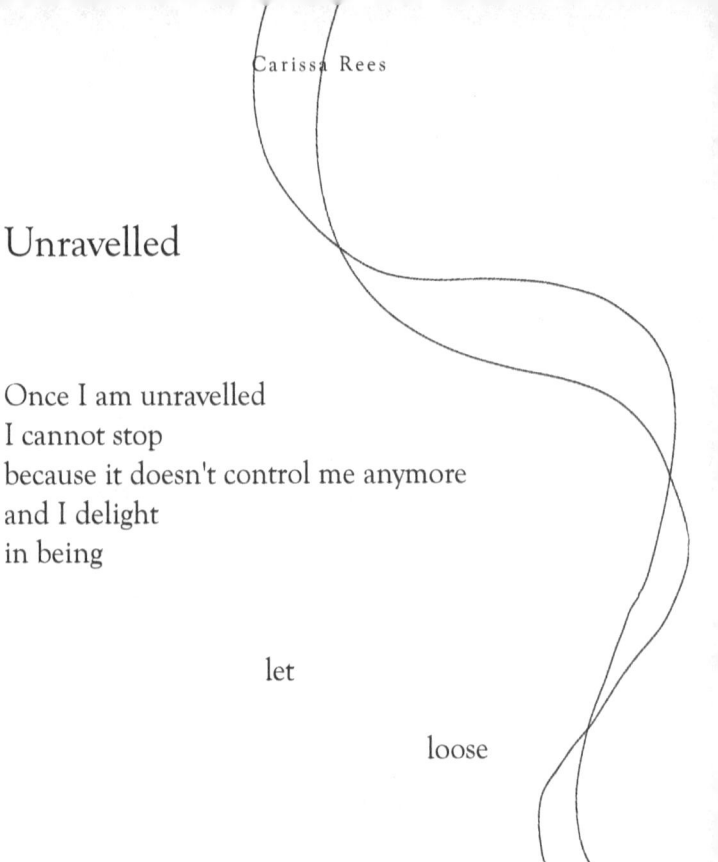

The Breaking of Myself

Balance along beams

I balance along beams
cartwheel across sand
sometimes i'm so happy
it seems
I must do a handstand
I love doing the things
that I did
as a kid

There are no answers

There is freedom in knowing
that I am not meant to know the answers

Taking up space

It all changed
when I chose to remain
in the flame

the longer that I burn
the more the wax melts

and the more the wax melts
the more space I can fill

The Breaking of Myself

My fear doesn't yield power

My fear doesn't yield power
over me
anymore

this longing for death
makes my longing to live
even stronger

and yes I am afraid
but fear is only the awareness
that I am about to do something
that fear itself is afraid of

Immersed in sunlight

Being immersed in sunlight is warmth
it's breath on my skin
it's worries leaving

It's the taste of salt
and the colour orange
on my eyelids

It's being kissed on the forehead
it's nutrients for the soul
and being nurtured

It's being immersed in beauty
it's being told i'm worthy
i'm seen and I can rest now

It's refuge, it's safety
it's being held
by someone who loves me

Raindrops

Just like raindrops
I have found my place
by falling
        and landing
  somewhere good
despite all the not knowings

The Breaking of Myself

Underlying sadness

There's an underlying sadness in everything I do
from the way I tie my hair
to the way I speak with you

there's an overlapping scare
in all these desires
and in what I choose to share

most of all there's an intertwining pain
that's detrimental to my care
to my brain

and are others going to see through?
or is it up to me
to allow them to?

The Breaking of Myself

Acknowledgments

It has not been easy opening up and sharing what's inside of me with people in my own life let alone to publish some of my most deepest thoughts and insecurities. I have been learning to be vulnerable and that letting myself be seen can be a beautiful thing. Publishing these poems is just another meaningful step in my journey. I would love to express my gratitude to Michaela Clements, Harley Bigger, Cora Brotherton, April Feng, Sophie Green and Sofie Michaelson.

I'm also deeply thankful to the first readers of my work for their thoughtful feedback and encouragement, including Bella Carney, Jessica Cignarella, Zoe Gee, Ewan Heycock, Kerstin Jenkinson, Keisha Liem, Deborah May, and Petro Prifti.

Special thanks to David Tensen, author of *The Wrestle*, whose insightful thoughts and advice have been invaluable

I am forever grateful to my parents, Peter and Naomi for always supporting my endeavours and encouraging me to pursue my dreams.

This book simply wouldn't exist without the encouragement and love I have received.

Praise for *The Breaking of Myself*

"Carissa's poems bring her unique voice to important and relatable aspects of the human experience. She wisely and bravely writes about the things we forget to notice and the things we hesitate to share. These poems will nudge you to treasure your life and open your heart."
– Deborah May

"This is a beautifully crafted masterpiece. From forms of healing to the true break of a heart, Carissa Rees really knows how to write strong poems that can connect with a soul."
– Keisha Liem

"The words here held a rawness that I think sounds a lot like human thought. It's vulnerable and honest. It's touching things that need to be touched."
– Bella Carney

"Carissa's words are full of hope and peace. The honesty and vulnerability really allow you to revisit your own emotions in a beautiful, soft way."
– Jessica Cignarella

Carissa Rees is a young poet living on the Sunshine Coast, Australia. She spent six months living in Northern Ireland, an experience that deepened her love for quiet places and reflective moments. She feels most at home in nature: walking through the forest, sitting by the ocean, or simply being still. With a voice that's both sincere and insightful, she invites readers to embrace the complexity of life's emotional journey.

Facebook, Instagram, TikTok and Youtube are all under the username @carissareespoetry

Scan with smartphone to
follow me on Instagram

www.ingramcontent.com/pod-product-compliance
Lightning Source LLC
Chambersburg PA
CBHW030232100526
44583CB00013BA/889

"With the lightness of a comic strip, *Misbehaving in Maine* strikes with the impact of a sweeping and poignant novel. It's a book to revisit throughout life. In quick-moving episodes, Daniel Williams ushers us through the perils of childhood and brotherhood, making us cry, gasp, quake in terror, and laugh until we cry again. The author's brilliant visual artwork, as essential to the text as are the luminous plates to the works of William Blake, conveys the key emotional truths of his scenes with deceptive simplicity. In words and phrases wielded with virtuoso skill, Williams addresses the biggest stuff: sin, faith, belief, love, grace, and forgiveness. We cannot but love our guide, together with whom we are hopelessly doomed and hopelessly blessed."

Frederic S. Durbin, author of *A Green and Ancient Light* and *The Country Under Heaven*

"Reading the life of young Dan is a little like reading one of those Irish stories. You know, the ones that make you laugh out loud while something horrible happens. Little Brother Dan: 'I like dinosaurs.' Big Brother Joe: 'I like them more—' Dan: 'I hate you!' You know it's wrong to laugh, but you cannot help yourself. Finally, the wise mother enters the scene and helps both boys at least half-learn how to misbehave less in Maine. There *will* be blood. And pee, atomic diarrhea, rotting human flesh, and the insides of various dead animals.

"Prepare to laugh and to thank God that you were not the parents of young Dan. He is a 'man of action' who remembers with surprising clarity, honesty, and great humor his many missteps on the way to being a responsible human being. He makes things happen. Sometimes to his life-long humiliation. We suffer with him—laughing all the way. We are rooting for you, Dan, that you will learn the other halves of all those half-learned lessons."

Dr. Shirley Kilpatrick, Professor Emerita of English and Humanities, Geneva College

"Daniel Williams' memoir is not for the faint of heart. It is a perfect mix of cruelty and tenderness, a savagely endearing *Bildungsroman*, a cry of hilarious despair, a rebellion against mercy and stagnation, a series of childhood lessons that teach and punish in equal measure, a glimpse into a darkly comic world of misfits and reluctant heroes where time flows differently, pausing only for adventure. This is a beautiful book, nostalgic and pure, that captures flawlessly the splendor and the sadness of childhood."

Dayana Stetco, author of *The Loneliness Pill and Other Plays*

"Each episode is hilarious, poignant, and devastatingly exact about our essential humanity because Dan's wit, like all great cultural critics who happen to be comedic geniuses, sees the extraordinary in the mundane. I think Dan can see—much like Flannery O'Connor sees—the essential distortions that are weirdly present in all of us, and his illustrations—again, much like O'Connor's cartoons—use simplified but exaggerated shapes to reinforce his lessons, lessons that are wise and true."

Dr. Lynda Szabo, Professor of English & Humanities, Geneva College

"Why can't you write something nice?"

Mom

"I've got no patience for stupid."

Dad